I CAN READ ABOUT BASKETBALL

Written by Richard Harris
Illustrated by John Milligan

Troll Associates

Back in 1891, Dr. James Naismith had a problem. All winter long, his football and baseball players had nothing to do. They needed a new indoor sport!

Then he had an idea. He nailed a peach basket to the balcony at each end of the gym. "Try to throw the ball into the basket," he called. And that's how the game of basketball was born!

Today, basketball is played all over the world. Tall people, short people, boys, and girls play basketball.

You can have lots of fun playing basketball if you understand what the game is all about. Here are some basketball words and terms that may help you . . .

EQUIPMENT: You can play basketball in regular clothes, but if you belong to a team you may want to wear a uniform. A basketball player wears shorts, a sleeveless jersey, high socks, and sneakers. And don't forget the basketball. You can't play the game without it.

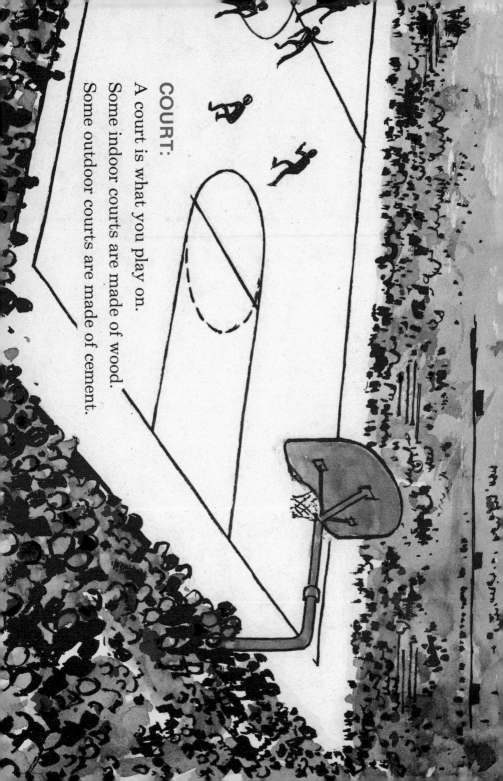

COURT:
A court is what you play on.
Some indoor courts are made of wood.
Some outdoor courts are made of cement.

BASKETS: Today's baskets look very different from peach baskets. The basket is a net, made of string. It is connected to a metal rim or hoop. The baskets are usually ten feet above the court.

BACKBOARD:
The basket is connected to a backboard. It is sometimes best to bounce the basketball off the backboard to make it fall through the net.

TEAM: A basketball team has five players: a center, two guards, and two forwards. Most basketball players are tall. But, if you are a fast runner, a good ball-handler, and a good shooter, it does not matter how tall you are.

CENTER:
The center is usually
the tallest player
on the team. The
center must be
good at jumping
and shooting.

FORWARD: The forwards try to score points for their team. They must be quick runners and good shooters.

GUARD:

The guards try to get the ball away from the other team. They also try to score points. Sometimes a guard waves his arms, and makes noises when he tries to get the ball away from the other team.

JUMP BALL: A jump ball starts the game. The centers meet at mid-court. The ball is tossed between them. They leap into the air, and they try to tap the ball to their teammates.

DRIBBLE: One way to get the ball toward the basket is to dribble it. When you dribble the ball, you bounce it up and down with your hand.

PASS: Another way to get the ball to the basket is to pass it to one of your teammates. A good pass to use is the chest pass. Hold the ball close to your chest and push it away with two hands.

FAKE: A good ball-handler knows how to fool the other team. Sometimes a ball-handler will look one way, and pass the ball the other way. This is called a fake.

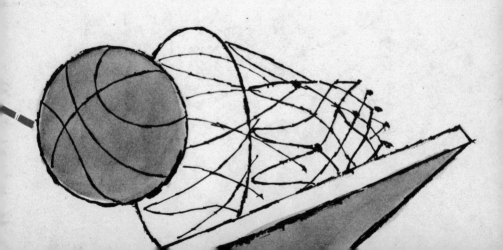

SHOOT:

To shoot the ball
means to send it flying
through the air
toward the basket.
It does not mean
that you take a gun
and shoot the ball.

JUMP SHOT:

One way to shoot the ball
is to take a jump shot.
Crouch, or bend, close
to the floor. Then
spring into the air
as you toss the ball
toward the basket.

HOOK SHOT: To make a hook shot, sweep the ball over your head with one hand and send it flying toward the basket.

SWISH:

When your shot
falls through the net
without touching the rim or backboard,
it goes *SWISH!* Listen carefully . . .
maybe you'll hear it.

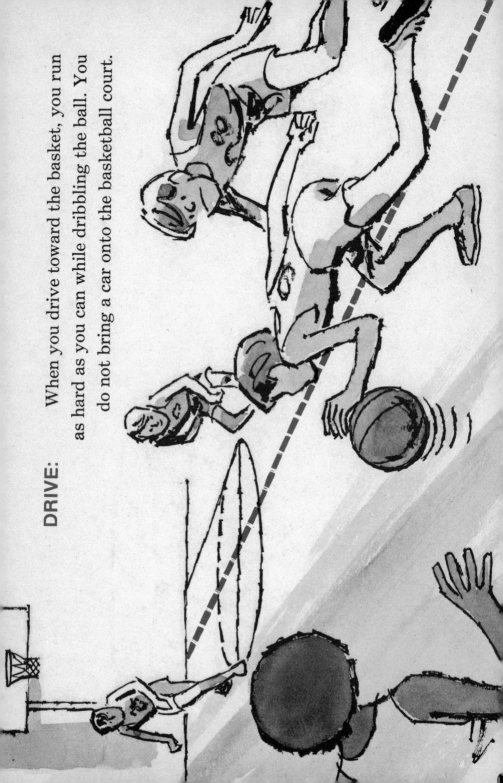

DRIVE: When you drive toward the basket, you run as hard as you can while dribbling the ball. You do not bring a car onto the basketball court.

PIVOT: Sometimes, when you are dribbling the ball, you want to change direction quickly. Try a pivot. Keep one foot on the floor, and whirl around.

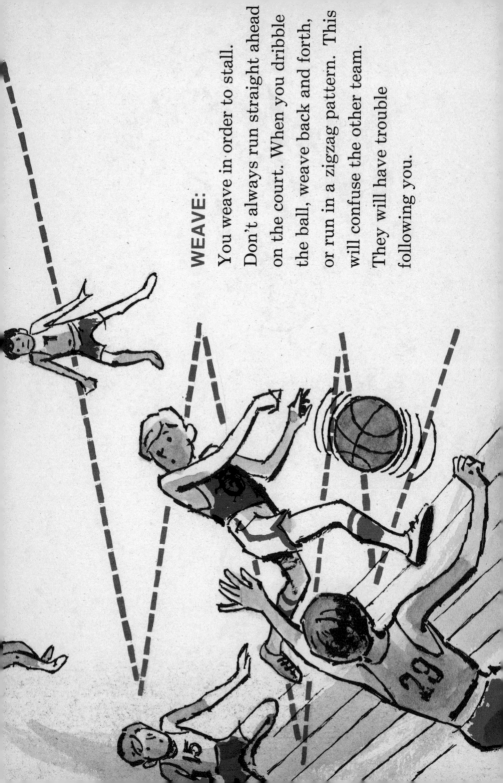

WEAVE:
You weave in order to stall. Don't always run straight ahead on the court. When you dribble the ball, weave back and forth, or run in a zigzag pattern. This will confuse the other team. They will have trouble following you.

TRAVELING:

Running with the ball in your hands is called traveling. If you are caught traveling, your team loses the ball.

FREEZING THE BALL:
When people on your team keep passing the ball to each other for a long time, it is called freezing the ball. When you freeze the ball, the other team cannot get it.

OUT-OF-BOUNDS:

A ball that is knocked off the court is said to be out-of-bounds. If you knock it off the court, the other team gets the ball.

POP!

DEAD BALL and LIVE BALL:
When a ball is not in play,
it is called a dead ball.
When a ball is dribbled, passed, or shot,
it is called a live ball.

TRIPLE THREAT:

Try to get into the triple threat position
when you have the ball.

Lean forward with your knees bent,
put one foot forward,
and hold the ball with two hands
close to your chest.

From this position, you are always
ready to pass, dribble, or shoot.

FIELD GOAL:

A field goal is a shot that goes through the net. It is worth two points. It is also called a basket or "sinking the ball."

DUNK:

If you are very tall, or if you can jump high, you may be able to dunk the ball. When you dunk the ball, you leap up and put it right into the basket. A dunk is also called a stuff.

REBOUND: If the other team misses the basket, don't just stand there . . . grab the rebound! Grab the ball when it bounces off the rim or backboard.

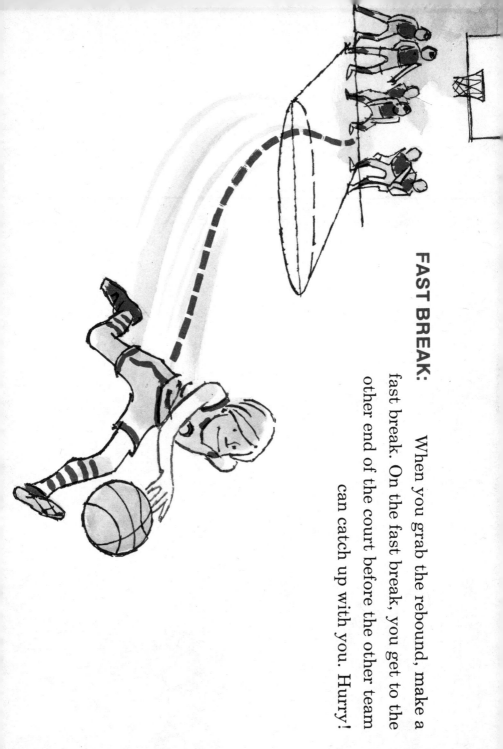

FAST BREAK:

When you grab the rebound, make a fast break. On the fast break, you get to the other end of the court before the other team can catch up with you. Hurry!

BLOCKED SHOT: If you keep the other team from scoring, by blocking or hitting their shots away from the basket, you will be a very valuable member of your team!

FOUL:

Holding, tripping,
and pushing other players
is against the rules.
When you break a rule, you commit
a foul. If you make too many
fouls, you are out of the game.

FOUL SHOT:

When you foul another player, that player is sometimes awarded, or given, a foul shot. This means the player gets to stand near the basket and take a free throw. All that your team can do is stand around and watch.

OFFENSE and DEFENSE:

When your team has the ball, you are playing offense. When your team does not have the ball, you are playing defense. In a fast-action game like basketball, offense and defense change very quickly.

ZONE DEFENSE: On defense, you might try a zone to keep the other team away from your basket. In a zone, the entire team moves as one unit to stop the other team from scoring.

MAN-TO-MAN:

On man-to-man defense, you guard one player throughout the entire game. It is your job to watch that player closely and to stay with him wherever he goes.

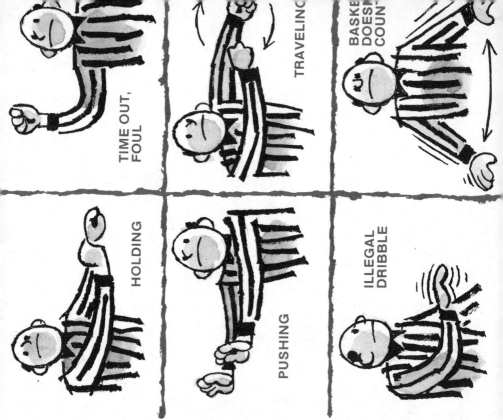

TIME OUT,
FOUL

TRAVELING

BASKET
DOESN'T
COUNT

HOLDING

PUSHING

ILLEGAL
DRIBBLE

REFEREES: Basketball referees are also called officials. They make sure that players obey the rules. When a player breaks the rules, a referee uses hand signals to show what the player did wrong.

COACH: The coach is in charge of the team. A coach decides what plays or strategy will be used during the game. Everyone is supposed to listen!

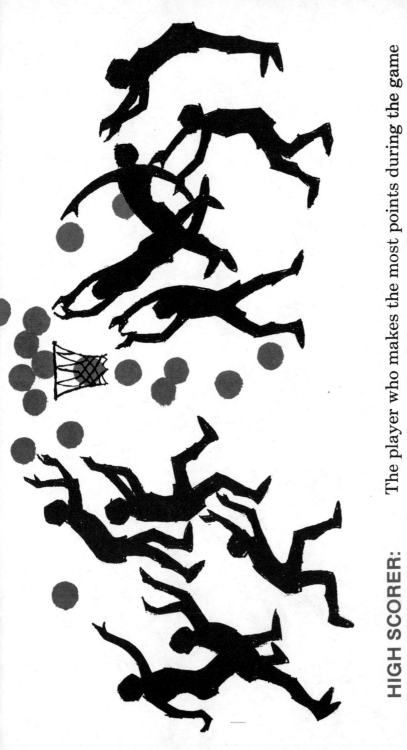

HIGH SCORER: The player who makes the most points during the game is the high scorer. Lots of practice will help you become a high scorer.

MVP

The MVP is the Most Valuable Player. The Most Valuable Player is usually the one who has done the most for the team throughout the season.

Now that you know what basketball is all about . . . . go out and play! Someday, maybe you'll be the high scorer or the Most Valuable Player on your team!